The Surrender of Cornwallis

by Ann Heinrichs

Content Adviser: James Kirby Martin, Ph.D.,
Distinguished University Professor of History,
University of Houston

Reading Adviser: Rosemary G. Palmer, Ph.D.,
Department of Literacy, College of Education,
Boise State University

Compass Point Books ✦ Minneapolis, Minnesota

Compass Point Books
3109 West 50th Street, #115
Minneapolis, MN 55410

Visit Compass Point Books on the Internet at *www.compasspointbooks.com*
or e-mail your request to *custserv@compasspointbooks.com*

On the cover: Detail from John Trumbull's 1781 painting *The Surrender of Lord Cornwallis
at Yorktown*

Managing Editor: Catherine Neitge
Page Production: Bobbie Nuytten
Photo Researcher: Svetlana Zhurkin
Cartographer: XNR Productions, Inc.
Library Consultant: Kathleen Baxter

Creative Director: Keith Griffin
Editorial Director: Carol Jones

Library of Congress Cataloging-in-Publication Data
Heinrichs, Ann.
  The surrender of Cornwallis / by Ann Heinrichs.
     p. cm.—(We the people)
  Includes bibliographical references and index.
  Audience: Grades 4–6.
  ISBN-13: 978-0-7565-2462-3 (library binding)
  ISBN-10: 0-7565-2462-8 (library binding)
  1. Yorktown (Va.)—History—Siege, 1781—Juvenile literature. I. Title. II. Series.
  E241.Y6H45 2007
  973.3'37—dc22   2006027093

TABLE OF CONTENTS

THE WORLD TURNED UPSIDE DOWN

Snarly and sullen, the soldiers slammed their guns down in a heap. It almost seemed they wanted to smash the guns to bits. The lines of surly soldiers stretched for more than a mile. All through the long afternoon, they marched up to Surrender Field in Yorktown, Virginia, to give up their arms. Though they were dressed in brand-new uniforms, they marched out of step in sloppy, undisciplined lines.

It's no wonder these soldiers were so glum. They were proud British troops suffering the shame of defeat. For weeks in 1781, they had been trapped in Yorktown. With no escape by land or sea, they were bombarded by General George Washington's forces.

Washington's Continental Army troops were not as well-dressed, well-trained, or well-fed as the British troops. But their hearts were in the fight. The 13 American colonies had had enough of Great Britain and its monarch, King

4

The redcoated British surrendered to the Americans on October 19, 1781.

George III. The colonists were waging the Revolutionary War for independence from British rule. Though the war dragged on for almost seven years, Washington's men clung to their vision of freedom.

At last, the British commander, General Charles Cornwallis, gave in. The Battle of Yorktown had broken him, and he surrendered on October 19, 1781. This was the last major battle of the Revolutionary War. Soon the new

Troops and ships surrounded British soldiers as they surrendered to the Americans.

United States would form its own government and take its place among the nations of the world.

    The surrender was depressing for Cornwallis' troops. As professional soldiers, they had every reason to believe they'd win the war. They couldn't understand how such a ragged army had beaten them. After handing over their guns, they headed off to prisoner-of-war camps. As they marched along in shame and dishonor, it is said that they played a tune called "The World Turned Upside Down."

A DANGEROUS MOVE

A long chain of events led up to Cornwallis' surrender at
Yorktown. English settlers had sailed to North America in
1607 and established the first English colony at Jamestown,

Early colonists prepared to build a fort at Jamestown, Virginia.

Virginia. Over the years, more and more settlers arrived. Some came to escape religious persecution. Others hoped to become wealthy or embark on new adventures. Eventually, the settlers formed 13 colonies under English rule.

In farming communities, the colonists raised vegetables, grains, tobacco, and cotton. Boys helped their fathers plow the fields, harvest the crops, and shoe the horses. Women and girls spun cotton and wool into yarn on spinning wheels. With the yarn, they wove cloth to make clothes. Candles, soap, and other necessities were all made by hand. In the winter, people huddled around fireplaces or potbellied, wood-burning stoves to keep warm.

Life in cities and towns was flourishing, too. Great ships sailed into colonial ports bearing tea, sugar, paper, and other goods from Great Britain. Along the cobblestone streets, merchants and craftspeople built thriving businesses. Philadelphia in the Pennsylvania Colony and Boston in the Massachusetts Colony became important colonial cities. In Philadelphia, Benjamin Franklin published the

Colonial women made their own cloth after spinning cotton and wool to make yarn.

Pennsylvania Gazette, which became a leading newspaper in the colonies.

By the 1760s, Great Britain was in debt after a long war with France. To raise money, Britain began making the colonists pay higher and higher taxes. The colonists felt they should have a voice in how they were governed—including how they were taxed. Angry colonists began to shout "No

9

taxation without representation!"

Britain sent troops to keep the colonists in line. Colonists resented the Redcoats, as they called the British soldiers. It was only a matter of time until violence erupted.

In the Boston Massacre of 1770, Redcoats fired on an angry mob of Americans, killing five people. In 1773, to protest a tax on tea, colonists boarded three British ships in Boston Harbor and dumped chests of tea overboard. This was called the Boston Tea Party. Finally, on April 19, 1775, shots rang out in Lexington and Concord in the Massachusetts Colony. After the smoke had cleared, several colonists lay dead. The Revolutionary War had begun, and the colonists prepared for the challenges that lay ahead.

Representatives from all the colonies formed the Continental Congress. These decision makers created the Continental Army, with George Washington as commander in chief. It wasn't easy to put together a fighting force. Many of Washington's soldiers were drawn from local militias.

British troops fought American colonists during the Boston Massacre.

They were volunteer bands of fighters ranging in age
from 15 to 60.

The next step was to make an exciting announce-
ment. On July 4, 1776, the Continental Congress issued the
Declaration of Independence. It declared that the colonies

11

Colonists in Philadelphia cheered as the Declaration of Independence was read.

were no longer under British control. Instead, they were the independent United States of America.

Declaring independence was a bold and dangerous move. If the revolution failed, Britain would probably execute many who took part in it. The colonists had to fight, and they had to win.

FRANCE TO THE RESCUE

In the early years of the Revolutionary War, most of the fighting took place in the Northern colonies. In 1776, thousands of British troops landed in New York City. They spread out, battling the colonists in New York, New Jersey, and Pennsylvania. The British had a powerful navy, too. Its warships wreaked havoc on the colonies' coastal cities.

General Washington began to realize that his army needed outside help. His soldiers would not be able to

British troops occupied New York City during the entire war.

hold up against the Redcoats. Soon France came to Washington's aid.

By joining the colonists, France could strike another blow against Britain. The two countries had been enemies for years. Many Frenchmen loved the idea of liberty, too. They hated being ruled by their king, just as the colonists resented Great Britain's king.

At first, a few French volunteers came to America to help the colonists. One was the Marquis de Lafayette, who arrived in 1777. Only 19 years old, Lafayette told Congress he believed in the American cause. He would even work for free if he could join Washington's army. Impressed, Congress gave him the rank of major general

Marquis de Lafayette

and assigned him to Washington's staff. Lafayette proved to be a courageous leader and fighter. He even used his own money to buy food and clothes for his soldiers. He and Washington would become lifelong friends.

Meanwhile, American diplomats were trying to persuade France to sign a treaty of alliance with the new United States. At last, in February 1778, France agreed. It would send soldiers, sailors, money, and supplies to help the Americans win their freedom. The French would later play a major role in defeating Cornwallis at Yorktown and ending the Revolutionary War.

Benjamin Franklin helped persuade the French king to aid the colonists.

THE WAR TURNS SOUTH

After France joined the colonists' side, the British began to get uneasy. Winning the war might be harder than they had thought. It was time for a new plan.

By the end of 1778, the war in the Northern colonies

The June 1778 Battle of Monmouth was the last major engagement in the North.

16

was deadlocked. Neither side could get a clear advantage over the other. The British decided to focus on the Southern colonies, especially Georgia, North and South Carolina, and Virginia. The British figured they needed to capture port towns along those colonies' coasts. Then it would be easy to get supplies sent by ship from New York City, the British headquarters.

Washington had his hands full in the North. So the Continental Congress put General Benjamin Lincoln in charge of defending the Southern colonies. He would face the forces of Sir Henry Clinton, commander in chief of the British army and navy.

Things did not go well for the American troops. Clinton's forces captured the port city of Savannah, Georgia. Then in 1780, Clinton attacked Charleston, South Carolina. Charleston was a major seaport and the South's biggest city. General Lincoln and his men defended Charleston the best they could, but it was not enough. They lost the city to the British.

Savannah fell to the British in late 1778, followed by Charleston in 1780.

Charleston was the costliest loss in the war so far.
More than 5,000 colonial soldiers were captured. And an
insult was added to the loss. According to war customs
at the time, a defeated army was granted the "honors of
war." That meant they could surrender with their col-
ors, or regimental flags, flying—a sign of their honor

and fighting spirit. But Clinton wouldn't allow Lincoln's troops to do this. The American general's men had to surrender with their flags rolled up on their poles and covered. Later, at Yorktown, this insult would not be forgotten.

Benjamin Lincoln

Delighted with his victories, Clinton returned to New York City. His second in command, General Charles Cornwallis, was left behind to lead the British forces in the South. At the time, this seemed like a good decision. But for the British, it was the first step toward disaster.

CORNWALLIS ON THE RUN

Charles Cornwallis was a British nobleman. He was addressed as Lord Cornwallis because he held the title Second Earl Cornwallis.

He was just 17 when he joined the British army. After serving in Germany, Cornwallis became a member of Parliament, Britain's law-making body. In Parliament, he opposed Great Britain's harsh taxes on the colonists. He was even a bit sympathetic to the

Charles Cornwallis

20

colonists' complaints. Nevertheless, when the Revolutionary War broke out, he volunteered to fight against the rebels.

In 1776, Cornwallis arrived in New York with 2,500 British troops. He fought Washington's forces in New Jersey in 1776 and in Pennsylvania in 1777. Now in 1780, Cornwallis faced his biggest challenge.

Cornwallis' orders were to make sure North and South Carolina were firmly under British control. Once this was done, he could move on to Virginia. Things did not go smoothly for Cornwallis. He did win a great victory in the Battle of Camden, South Carolina, in August 1780. But it was followed by two costly defeats—the battles of Kings Mountain in October 1780 and Cowpens in January 1781.

His forces badly mangled, Cornwallis retreated into North Carolina. There he faced colonial troops under General Nathanael Greene. The two armies chased each other around North Carolina, engaging in minor battles. Greene's soldiers just never seemed to quit. As Greene said, "We fight, get beat, rise, and fight again." Finally, in

The Battle at Guilford Courthouse is considered one of the most important of the war.

March 1781, the two sides met in the Battle of Guilford

Courthouse.

"I never saw such fighting since God made me,"

Cornwallis said of this battle against Greene and the American soldiers. The British won, but it was a bloody, costly victory. Cornwallis then moved his bedraggled troops to Wilmington, on the North Carolina coast. There they could rest and recover.

Now Cornwallis made a crucial decision. Contrary to his orders, he did not remain in the Carolinas to keep them in British hands. Instead, he decided to move into Virginia.

When Cornwallis' superior, Sir Henry Clinton, heard about this, he was outraged. Had he known what Cornwallis was up

Nathanael Greene served during the entire war and is considered one of George Washington's best officers.

23

Henry Clinton

to, Clinton said, "I should certainly have endeavoured to stop you, as I … consider such a move likely to be dangerous to our interests in the Southern Colonies."

Moving into Virginia was dangerous indeed. Just seven months later, the British army would suffer its most humiliating and decisive defeat.

THE TRAP IS SET

By early 1781, George Washington was discouraged with the war. Neither side seemed close to winning. With the war now six years old, public support was beginning to sag. "The people are discontented," Washington wrote to a friend.

Nearly 25,000 Americans died in military service during the Revolutionary War.

The Continental Army was in bad shape, too. Congress was not giving the army enough money for uniforms and supplies. "It is equally certain," wrote Washington, "that our Troops are approaching fast to nakedness and that we have nothing to cloath them with. That our Hospitals are without medicines, and our Sick without Nutriment."

Washington still wanted to fight the British in the north. Then he learned that Cornwallis was moving into Virginia, and he called on his trusty French ally, the Marquis de Lafayette. The young Frenchman was to defend Virginia against the British forces.

All through Virginia, Lafayette harassed Cornwallis' troops. "The boy [Lafayette] cannot escape me," Cornwallis wrote. But it was really the other way around. Lafayette was pursuing Cornwallis toward the Virginia coast. Reaching Yorktown, Cornwallis dug in. His men built a series of fortifications around Yorktown, at the mouth of the York River. They also built defenses across the river on

Lafayette rallied his troops in pursuit of Cornwallis.

a little point of land called Gloucester.

Meanwhile, things were looking up for General Washington. In July 1781, he was joined by French general Jean-Baptiste Rochambeau and 5,500 French soldiers. Their combined forces were getting ready to go after British commander Clinton in New York. But in August, Washington

27

Jean-Baptiste Rochambeau

heard even more good news. A fleet of French ships under Admiral François de Grasse was headed to Virginia. This was Washington's chance to trap Cornwallis. Instead of having to face these British troops on yet another battlefield, he could keep them trapped and wear them out. With no way to get fresh troops, ammunition, or even food, the British were sure to fall.

Washington quickly sent a message to Lafayette. He was to block the British by land so they couldn't retreat. To distract Clinton, Washington left some soldiers behind in New York to act as if they were preparing for an attack. Then Washington and Rochambeau slipped away and

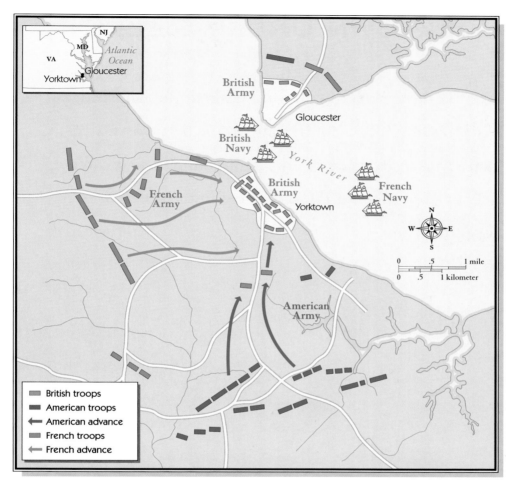

The British were surrounded by American and French troops and French ships.

marched south toward Virginia. When they arrived on
September 28, Admiral de Grasse was already blockading
Yorktown by sea. It was only a matter of time before the
trap snapped shut on Charles Cornwallis.

29

YORKTOWN UNDER SIEGE

The Battle of Yorktown is often called the Siege of Yorktown. A siege is different from a battle on an open field. In a siege, a city or fort is surrounded so it can't get supplies. Then it is bombarded until its defenses break down.

The Siege of Yorktown *was painted for the French king in 1784 by Louis N. Van Blarenberghe.*

That's what happened at Yorktown. Cornwallis had built 10 small forts as a line of defense. When Washington arrived, his men began digging a long trench facing Cornwallis' position. By October 9, the trench was done. Then cannons were put in place alongside it. Hunkered in their trenches, the soldiers would be safe from enemy fire.

For two days, cannons battered away at Cornwallis' fortifications. One British soldier wrote: "One could … not avoid the horribly many cannon balls … many were badly injured and mortally wounded by the fragments of bombs, … their arms and legs severed or themselves struck dead."

Cornwallis was in a panic. He had about 8,300 troops. But he was surrounded by a combined force of 17,600 men on land and sea. He was running low on gunpowder, cannonballs, and food. Exhausted and hungry, his soldiers could barely go on. Where were reinforcements? Where were more supplies? General Clinton had promised to send a ship with 5,000 more British troops. But the port was blocked, and they would arrive too late.

General George Washington directed the action at Yorktown.

Meanwhile, Washington had his men dig a second trench, even closer to Cornwallis' line. On October 14, French and American troops stormed two key British forts.

The end was in sight as American troops overwhelmed a British fort in 10 minutes.

Cornwallis was desperate. On the night of October 16, he
gathered some troops and supplies into boats. They tried
to escape across the York River to Gloucester. But a fierce
windstorm forced them back, and they couldn't go on.
Cornwallis finally faced the fact that all was lost.

THE GLORIOUS EVENT

On the cool, crisp morning of October 17, 1781, George Washington's troops observed a curious sight. High on a mound above the scarred battleground stood a drummer boy, tapping out a rhythmic beat. Then a British officer appeared, waving a white handkerchief. It was the sign of surrender.

An American soldier ran out, blindfolded the British officer, and led him to General Washington. The officer bore a letter from Cornwallis saying: "I propose a cessation of hostilities … and that two officers may be appointed by each side, to meet at Mr. Moore's house, to settle terms for the surrender of the posts of York and Gloucester."

Augustine Moore owned a large farmhouse in Yorktown. On October 18, two officers from each side met there. For hours, they hammered out the Articles of Capitulation, the surrender agreement.

Washington offered rather generous terms. British

A British officer signaled surrender on October 17, 1781.

officers could keep their side arms, and officers and soldiers
could keep their personal belongings. Cornwallis and other
ranking officers were allowed to go home or to a British-

Famed photographer William Henry Jackson took a picture of the Moore house in 1903.

occupied American port. Soldiers would be sent to prison camps in Virginia, Pennsylvania, and Maryland.

However, Washington insisted on one harsh point. He knew that in Charleston, American soldiers under General Lincoln had to surrender without the proper honors of war. Washington made sure to return the insult: "The same

British soldiers surrendered with their flags rolled up, without the honors of war.

Honors will be granted to the Surrendering Army as were granted to the Garrison of Charles Town." The British flags would not be allowed to fly.

At noon on October 19, the surrender ceremony began. Hundreds of curious citizens gathered to watch the spectacle. The American and French victors formed two long lines leading to a grassy meadow now called Surrender Field. On the left were the French troops, headed by Rochambeau. On the right were the Americans, with Washington striking a stately pose on horseback.

At 2 o'clock, the defeated army began marching in two lines between the victorious troops. As Washington had instructed, British flags were rolled up and covered. Each man tossed his gun and ammunition belt into a pile.

In a breach of military etiquette, Cornwallis refused to attend the ceremony, saying he was "indisposed." He sent his second in command, General Charles O'Hara. In a further insult, O'Hara tried to hand Cornwallis' sword of surrender to Rochambeau instead of Washington. Rochambeau refused to take it and pointed to Washington. But Washington, in turn, pointed to his second in command, Benjamin Lincoln, who took the sword.

Detail from Van Blarenberghe's 1785 painting Surrender at Yorktown

Washington later wrote a letter to the Continental Congress telling about the "glorious event." When the victory was announced in Philadelphia a few days later, cheering citizens poured into the streets. Cornwallis wrote to Clinton, his commander: "I have the mortification to inform your Excellency that I have been forced to

News of the surrender was announced to a jubilant crowd of Philadelphians.

… surrender the troops under my command … as prisoners of war to the combined forces of America and France."

The news of the surrender reached Great Britain in November. Soon the British government lost its will to continue the war. Not many battles were fought after 1781. In 1783, the Treaty of Paris formally ended the war and recognized American independence.

Inspired by the Americans, the French people went on to stage their own revolution in 1789. Cornwallis and Clinton spent the rest of their lives blaming each other for the failure at Yorktown. As for George Washington, he became the first president of the nation he fought so hard to create.

After the war, Cornwallis served in Ireland and India, where he died in 1805.

GLOSSARY

alliance—an agreement between nations or groups of people to work together

blockading—a military effort preventing goods from entering and leaving a region

capitulation—the act of surrender

Continental Congress—legislative assembly of delegates from the 13 colonies who met during and after the American Revolution; they issued the Declaration of Independence and framed the Articles of Confederation

deadlocked—at a standstill

diplomats—people who manage their countries' affairs with other nations

etiquette—rules of correct behavior

fortifications—buildings or walls built as military defenses

militias—groups of citizens organized to fight but who are not professional soldiers

reinforcements—additional troops that bring increased strength

DID YOU KNOW?

- Many colonists remained loyal to Great Britain during the Revolutionary War. They were called loyalists. Those who wanted independence were called patriots.

- It's said that Lord Frederick North, the British prime minister, took the news of the Yorktown defeat "as he would have taken a [musket] ball in the breast." He wrote in his diary: "Oh, God! It's all over."

- Yorktown had a population of almost 2,000 in 1750. Much of the town was destroyed in the Revolutionary War, and by 1790, only 661 people lived there.

- As a young man, Charles Cornwallis attended Great Britain's Eton College—an elite secondary school for boys—and Cambridge University.

- After the war, Jean-Baptiste Donatien de Vimeur, Comte de Rochambeau, returned to a military career in France. He at first backed the French Revolution, but later became upset with the excessive violence. Rochambeau was imprisoned and nearly executed.

IMPORTANT DATES

Timeline

1775	The Revolutionary War begins with the Battles of Lexington and Concord in Massachusetts.
1776	Colonists issue the Declaration of Independence.
1778	France joins the United States in its fight for independence.
1780	General Charles Cornwallis becomes commander of British forces in the South.
1781	Cornwallis surrenders to General George Washington at Yorktown, Virginia.
1783	Great Britain and the United States sign the Treaty of Paris, formally ending the Revolutionary War.

IMPORTANT PEOPLE

SIR HENRY CLINTON (c. 1738–1795)

Commander in chief of British forces during the Revolutionary War; he resigned his command in 1782 and returned to England, where he was blamed for the loss of the colonies

LORD CHARLES CORNWALLIS (1738–1805)

Leader of British troops in the South who surrendered to George Washington at Yorktown; he went on to have a diplomatic career

FRANÇOIS DE GRASSE (1722–1788)

French naval officer whose ships cut off British movement into and out of Yorktown; he was later defeated by the British in the West Indies and held prisoner for several months

MARQUIS DE LAFAYETTE (1757–1834)

French nobleman, soldier, and statesman whose French and American troops helped defeat Cornwallis at Yorktown; after the war he continued to support American interests during a long career in France; in 2002, he was named an honorary U.S. citizen, a rare honor

GEORGE WASHINGTON (1732–1799)

Commander in chief of the colonial forces during the Revolutionary War who became the first president of the United States

45

WANT TO KNOW MORE?

At the Library

Ferrie, Richard. *The World Turned Upside Down: George Washington and the Battle of Yorktown*. New York: Holiday House, 1999.

Harmon, Daniel E. *Lord Cornwallis, British General.* Philadelphia: Chelsea House, 2002.

Murphy, Jim. *A Young Patriot: The American Revolution as Experienced by One Boy.* New York: Clarion Books, 1996.

Parker, Lewis K. *Charles Cornwallis.* San Diego: Blackbirch Press, 2002.

On the Web

For more information on this topic, use FactHound.

1. Go to *www.facthound.com*

2. Type in this book ID: 0756524628

3. Click on the *Fetch It* button.

FactHound will find the best Web sites for you.

On the Road

Colonial National Historical Park

Yorktown Visitor Center

Colonial Parkway

Yorktown, VA 23690

757/898-2410

The Yorktown battlefield and sites in Yorktown that the British defended during the siege

Yorktown Victory Center and Museum

Route 1020

Yorktown, VA 23690

888/593-4682

Films, exhibits, and living-history demonstrations about the people and events involved with the Battle of Yorktown

Look for more We the People books about this era:

The Articles of Confederation

The Battle of Bunker Hill

The Battles of Lexington and Concord

The Bill of Rights

The Boston Massacre

The Boston Tea Party

The Declaration of Independence

The Electoral College

Great Women of the American Revolution

The Minutemen

Monticello

Mount Vernon

Paul Revere's Ride

The U.S. Constitution

Valley Forge

A complete list of We the People titles is available on our Web site: www.compasspointbooks.com

INDEX

About the Author

Ann Heinrichs is the author of more than 200 books for children and young
adults. She grew up in Fort Smith, Arkansas, and now makes her home in
Chicago. An avid traveler, Ann has journeyed through most of the United
States, as well as the Middle East, Africa, and East Asia.